T0046772

WAIL SONG

Wail Song:
wading in the water at the end of the world

by Chaun Webster

Black Ocean
Boston · Chicago

Black Ocean
P.O. Box 52030
Boston, MA 02205
blackocean.org

Cover Art and Design by Janaka Stucky| blackocean.org
Book Design by Chaun Webster
Book Layout by taylor d. waring | taylordwaring.com

ISBN: 978-1-939568-68-7
Library of Congress Control Number: 2022951890
Printed in Canada

FIRST EDITION

for Ocean Cade Morrison. your name was always a prayer, your breath, your impossible breathing, a gift.

CONTENTS

A WORD AT THE SO-CALLED "BEFORE"

if the *sea is history*, as Walcott tells us, then *Wail Song* is an attempt at beginning—
if we believe in such orderings of time—there, in the water, the abyssal. here in
these assemblages is a prolonged struggle to snatch something from the depths,
against the belief that nothing can be recovered, i no longer believe anything
can be recovered, and yet i cannot forgo the attempt. so here we are, in the
water, having jumped the *Pequod* and wading through and against antiblackness,
which is to say an apocalyptic extractive regime of world-making—all i see are
the ruins. *a billion black anthropocenes[1]*. all i see is an ecology at its end. let's start
there. with a whale, a hunted thing, a species that once lived on land and gave
it up (*we don't want no fucking country[2] neither*) hunted as soon as it comes up for
air. let's begin with that snatched breath, with an ocean from which, and over,
so much has been taken and deposited and for which the ramifications remain
without grammar. let's begin with new world blackness, the belly of the whale.
the catastrophic ends entangled with its emergence. the sentient folk on the
outside of the human who are designated by this signifier. *Wail Song* is a long
meditation, that aims at extended thinking and conversation with thinking at
the shoreline[3] of blackness, the nonhuman animal, the middle passage and
ecological disaster. it is a written gesture, in all of its uncertainty, of moving
toward the terror, desiring something beyond the terror, while not knowing if
anything lay on the other side of it. *Wail Song* is an attempt at care, with and
for those in what Christina Sharpe calls *the wake*. for if i cannot raise my dead,
and i suspect i cannot, then i will bear witness past the edge of ruin and will
wail this world till its end.

1. See Kathryn Yusoff, *A Billion Black Anthropocenes or None*. Minneapolis, University of Minnesota
Press, 2018.
2. See Dionne Brand, *Land to Light On*. Toronto, McClelland & Stewart, 1997.
3. See John E. Drabinski, *Glissant and the Middle Passage: Philosophy, Beginning, Abyss*. Minneapolis,
University of Minnesota Press, 2019.

"Who is this animal man?"

—Samuel R. Delaney, *Babel-17*

" . . . what is this black thing? Is it property? Is it human? Is it animal? Does it lack taxonomy? Is it nothing?"

—Calvin Warren, *Ontological Terror*

to be swallowed by a great fish
in the belly of the whale
at the end of the world
might be as good a place as any
to begin.

what does it mean to be in
the belly of the whale?
to be in the belly

                                        & the

whale.

this is meant to say
something about

being.

not only at the end of the
world
but being itself
and its zero . . .

which is to say
blackness.

somewhere in the water moves: a big fish. sounds like:
a catch. moves like: a hunted thing, its dark body

somewhere in the water. a big fish is a gold-
rush, loot, mined for the resource of its dark body.

somewhere in the water a big fish sounds like: sea-
monster, cetacean, from kētos. its dark body

somewhere in the water as a haunt, and the source
of modernity torn from its dark body.

somewhere in the water a big fish isn't a
big fish. it is trade, a ledger mark, its dark body

somewhere in the water as a metaphor, a fact
of capital registered from its dark body.

and there are bodies that are

mined—dis membered—distortions of distortion
(see Warren), situated solely as function.

not persons.

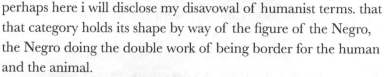

perhaps here i will disclose my disavowal of humanist terms. that
that category holds its shape by way of the figure of the Negro,
the Negro doing the double work of being border for the human
and the animal.

there are no persons here.

but we are getting ahead of ourselves. we are talking about bodies.

the whale

and in the belly of the whale.

pull the body close, right alongside you. it is
yours now. prepare the tools. sharpen them. the precious

parts are made so by extraction. remove what you
need. it is yours now. not a body, a precious

means to fetch a price. name it something phallic. it
is yours now. come, make a market of your precious

head matter. make a candle. light your way. it is
yours now. not: alive. a calculus of precious

trade. no body here. a lit dinner, a lantern
law. so many gallons. it is yours now. precious

stench. rank dominion. this corpse. it is yours now.
make your will so, as though, nothing here was precious.

i'm interested in impossibilities—like what it means to look squarely at the end—and then look beyond it. species impossibilities, such as breathing underwater. *nothing* is a new world liquid asset, it knows what it is to be under water. *nothing* knows what it is to be impossible—for death not to be an event but a state of being—to make a noise from within the wake. and what consideration can be made of a howl? the scream? noise emerging from the belly? how can one utter anything under the water?

PIP JUMPS THE *PEQUOD* TO MEET WITH JONAH IN THE BELLY OF AN UNSPECIFIED WHALE FOR DRINKS: MOVIE PITCH

so somewhere circling the dark continent rounding the expanse of that large mass of land out in the middle of the Indian Ocean—somewhere out on that water aboard the *Pequod* we got Pip. crew called him blackling and boy—sound small enough to not have a name, a kind of *fabricated presence*. yeah, Pip gets tired of being there . . . and not—a place like so many caskets—aboard some mobile graveyard. and Pip is thirsty, mouth so dry he think he might consume the sea, and so he jumps overboard. meanwhile Jonah been doing a short stint in the belly of an unspecified whale that happens to pick Pip up on his way to the seafloor and they get the talking over a couple of drinks. film concludes with the steady build of Pip and Jonah's riotous laughter over Nineveh, and the obsessions some men cannot seem to satiate, and the worlds they intend to never consider saving. cue music. fade to black . . .

my grandad knew the belly of the whale.

no jonah.

no summoning to collect the pieces of a world that

presumed death.

he knew the belly of the whale.

something in the depths

seen

but not seeing

or perhaps that is the error of a name.

animal.

human.

and that which stands between.

a ghost inside the leviathan.

his father rode it north to a perceived elsewhere.

surrounded by the water he drank himself to some kind of
beyond.

bod·y

/'bädē/

n.

1. a: the organized physical substance of an animal
or plant either living or dead: as

      (1): the material part or nature of a
human being

      (2): the dead organism : **CORPSE**

      (3): the person of a human being before
the law

  b: a human being : **PERSON**

there is no one body falling.

one is a modern fact
another kind of decomposition.

one is not a body
a discrete figure

one is

falling.

an assemblage

no

one

falling.

dark space carries a body
there is no one

an assemblage
a feast of falling.

one is not a body
one is a wail
fall(ing)

an assemblage. a dark space. carrying nothing
more than a body.

make the incision just below the hole. steady
your hand and sever the strip in two. remember,

you are cold, and this black mass after being cut
rightly may help your chilled flesh and bones remember

a former warmth. steel yourself and peel a blanket
or two. there are no thieves here. you must remember

dominion need not ask. wrap yourself in a sheet
of the black mass of flesh before you. remember,

this dark creature is a known quantity. something
measured: a candle's exchange value. remember

the righteousness of possession. slake your bitter
hunger until there is nothing to remember.

& sometimes the great fish is brought to court. its dark body cross-examined. & sometimes a body will change families or utterly disappear, mammalia being expanded or a fish-oil tax evaded. & sometimes whether you name a thing a great fish or a marine mammal, its dark body is still rendered. sometimes its flesh is made into a candle, something ignitable, the whole earth a mess of tinder.

W *or* an expression for the wail :: the whale :: which is to say water :: which is to say world

$$W w_{2(3)} h_2 \text{ or } \Phi_4 /_{2(3)}^+ \backslash_2 \text{ or } /_4$$

W, has four common forms. peel back the flesh. fold the layers. an architecture of muscle and bone. fold again. disaggregate the body—its many precincts. loop back. a corpus of sound. fold. another body. peel the flesh. shake together the bones. then apart. fold again. peel. until nothing is whole. nothing. just a world.

wherein the belly of the whale is misnomer,
the belly of the world.

that ship, my friends

whose bones
are these?

whose bones
are these

whose bones
are these?

a technology also

says something of
the body

of a mobile
graveyard.

whose bones
are these?

a technology also

that ship, my friends

say something of
the body:

whose bones
are these?

*the contraband was
jonah.*

now

says something of
the body

say something of
the body:

in the mobile
graveyard?

*was the first of recorded
smugglers!*

say something of
the body:

*was the first of recorded
smugglers!*

that ship, my friends

*the contraband was
jonah*

says something of
the body

whose bones
are these

bring the darkness of
blackness

that ship, my friends,

you

carrying

of a mobile
graveyard.

a technology also

that ship, my friends

at the mobile
graveyard

that ship, my friends

a technology also

brings the darkness of
blackness

at the mobile
graveyard.

*was the first of recorded
smugglers!*

at the mobile
graveyard?

a technology also

*was the first of recorded
smugglers!*

are

contraband.

27

whereas: some monsters can collapse their lungs, take their
residence among deep unknown fathoms, to breathe

they breach the space between worlds, liminal creatures.
something, everything other. other and they breathe.

whereas: a monstrous thing can be entangled, more
than single. multiple and without borders. breathe

and split the fiction of autonomy. breathe, there
is no distance from the water here. up, up and breathe

a kind of riotous practice, an anarchy
of breathing. whereas: monsters are hunted and breathe

at risk of being greeted by a cold harpoon.
whereas: revolt, because they can no longer breathe.

PIP JUMPS THE *PEQUOD* TO SNAG SOME PEARL FOR LUNCH BEFORE PLANNING A MUTINY: MOVIE PITCH

SCENE BEGINS WITH A BLACK SCREEN AND THE EMERGING SOUND OF A SLOW WHISTLE / *light builds* / audience sees Pip as he prepares to jump the *Pequod*. hungry, the crew believes there is something about Pip's body that makes it require less / *continued whistle* / that for Pip oxygen might not be essential—his animal body a hybrid thing that only surfaces occasionally. Pip dives into the water, descends a few fathoms down— hoop net in hand—to snag some pearl / *time lapse* /everyone aboard is a snarl, is set teeth, and wondering where their meal is since it has been hours / *continued whistle builds louder* / meanwhile Pip— mouthful of oysters—been below deck, seeing and not seen, fashioning a slow whistle into a howl . . .

wherein a body

(a) boards the Pequod. is rendered silent. negative.
(b) confuses the distance between object and subject.
(c) jumps ship.
(d) is mad. is madness. a mad black thing,
(e) is ungrateful for the ship, for the technology seemingly moving them
through the water.
(f) returns to the ship.
(g) folds the story. troubles the water.
(h) remakes what is in and outside of the ship. in and outside of itself.
(i) turns its interior into other things. a marine arrangement. a whole
world—with a wail—in the water.

to be in the belly
& the whale.

to be in the belly
& the whale.

to be in the belly

& the whale.

to be in the belly

& the whale.

in the b

& the whale

wail \wã(ə)l\

to begin. any place. might be a world. might be an end. to be swallowed in the world in the end might be as good an end as to be in the belly of the great fish to be at the end of the wail.

i am unsure where this is being written, what it means to
write a fragmented thing. to fragment a thing: a body, a spine,
text everywhere. i am unsure this is a trustworthy thing, in fact,
i am sure this is a thing not to be trusted. in the belly. at the end.
a body. and something more than a body.

take me to the water. there is something impossible about the land.

PIP JUMPS THE *PEQUOD* AFTER HALLUCINATING ABOUT THE HUMAN AND SUBSEQUENTLY GIVING UP ON LAND: MOVIE PITCH

it begins with a fever dream. Pip haunted by the ground he stands on, something terrifying about its sureness, its carcerality.   no, it begins somewhere in his torn-open throat—slit wide by a harpoon—camera panning each angle of Pip's neck as he wails: LOOK, A NEGRO! it begins with nothing: screen black—dark as the ocean floor.   no it begins with something: a body, itself both more and less than one, laying on the deck of the *Pequod* attempting to float—misjudging the surface for water—mistaking his lack of sinking for buoyancy. no it begins with a disavowal, of land, with Pip tasting that saltwater and it doing something like the opposite of stripping him of wings. Pip jumps the *Pequod*. no, it begins.

how have the dead entered here?

the
dead
are
monstrous
are
matter
are
your cognitive
foil
are . . .

preposition: the whale *on* the land. who gave up *on* the land.

preposition: to *be* under water.

read the bones, gather them together like printed matter, like a small city. go. further. past what you know, what is known. dead reckoning in the water. not lost. just outside the enclosure of a single body. go further. a league. 10 million years. a small thing. an ellipsis. and further. scour the seafloor for what has drowned. move in two directions at once. at once a body and not a body. nothing. build a cathedral of bones until that submerged nothingness—that body underwater—once again finds itself on what has come to be called land. inasmuch as being on land does not foreclose being under water. that body—on the land under water—picking its teeth with microfossils, some kind of remains, an enduring terror. impossibly possible.

and . . .

1

predicated on the belly

this is *the end of time, that shedding of the meaning of our bodies* this is a *speculative body* unthought and unrecognizable.

2 *relation*

here one would need to forget the human, one would need to relinquish an aspiring to humanness. here one would tell a story about the body & its movement through time as not only being conscripted to the ruin of its own flesh. an agnosticism toward a single metaphysics, one is not a believer, no. one is not interested in belief. here one would tell a story, the constellations of which would correspond with multiple subjectivities, always corresponding, an animate entanglement of subject and object. an ecology where the wail :: the whale :: the water :: the world :: are not to be distinguished from the commodity they swallow whole.

3 *the belly of the boat*

hold me until i break. in the break, a wail.

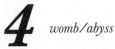 *womb/abyss*

perhaps there is no demand here, or no way to articulate it, beyond raising the dead, and yet, here i am talking about it as an event again, giving death a teleology. no. the ground has long been gone, something must be made of the water.

5

the belly of the world

everything has vibration, you know this now, the animate and the inanimate, everything. more than a species thinking. more than a small piece of something like hope to hold on to, there is no ground here. everything is vibrating, in the hold, you are not holding onto hope, you know this now. animate and inanimate points of vibration overlapping, folding, a palimpsest. you know this now, everything more than species, more than their categorical distinction, everything is vibrating, even in the belly & some days, you imagine this wail, song, giving utterance to something beyond the world.

6

world echoe

a wail will use only a tiny amount of air to produce its click in the depths of the world. at times only 100 microseconds, a flash of sound. it will travel faster here, in the underbelly, in the water. a wail, a flash of sound. in the depths of the world, sound is a . matter of sight. only a tiny amount of air. a wail, in the underbelly, in the water, in the black depths of the world. discordant and sounding.

7

the belly of the whale

so here we are both the whale and in its belly
because the human requires the hunt. perpetually.
modernity requires a network of bodies so large, a
ritual of blood so vast it can bring about a world.
and here we are in the nonworld of *the singularity, the
weather*, attempting to remember how to hold the
water—slippage—attempting to hold what cannot
be held what is *unavailable*, an ontology on the run.
here we are both the whale and in its belly working
ourselves deeper into the womb into the terror
wailing on our way into the abyss. here we are in search of
no salvation, there is no salvation, there is the whale and
its belly. and this may be an error, a failed attempt against
analogy, there are none. this, if nothing else, is an effort at
a grammar that will not look away, that will wail.

and . . . .

whale—wail body / black water / black whale / whale body / water body black / black body wail / whale water / wail water wail / whale black wail / body black / body / body / black / black / body / water / wail / wail / wail/ whale / whale / whale / water / water / wail / water / whale / body water wail black / water / water / water / water / water / black / water / body wail / water wail / black whale / wail / wail / wail / wail / wail / wail / as though the body of the whale were a body were a being were a black . . . being in the water in an other world. wail and let the eruption from the body rend the world.

and god created great whales, and every living creature
that moveth.

what is it to take seriously that *some lives are not lived in the world that the world lives in*? what is it for a life to be lived underground?

underwater?

the progenitors of the whale did not live their lives underwater.

whales

that is before they were whales

whales before they were the swallowers of jonah before they were the monsters of the sea, big fish of the old testament. whales before, the before-whales walked on dry land, spent time as a species in the above.

whales

before monsters of the sea
were beasts of the earth.

and somewhere for cumulative reasons that are merely speculated on, the whale before the whale gave up on land, the before-whales gave up on a former sense of world to the extent that we imagine the beast has world.

somewhere in an evolutionary expanse of time the before-whales took a dip or perhaps a dive from which they did not emerge.
the bios embraced another narrative
another world.

and it is these evolved bodies,
these fugitive bodies that are hunted.

and it is these creatures, these great moving bodies in the deep, these bodies that learned to hold their breath which is to say learned to circulate the oxygen, learned to make of the oxygen a body, these evolved bodies are hunted as soon as they surface to breathe.

hunted as though the hunters were seeking to evacuate the earth of air, of breathing.

some lives are not lived in the world that the world lives in.

and to the extent that one

a sum i hold at length

believes that there is a god that creates
great moving bodies of the deep
in a shattered world
not meant to hold the capacity for their breathing

to the extent that that is so,
those great moving bodies,
made of oxygen,
made of breathing,
those evolved bodies of the deep
might consider diving again,

might end *the world that the world lives in,*
the world that requires they relinquish their breathing.

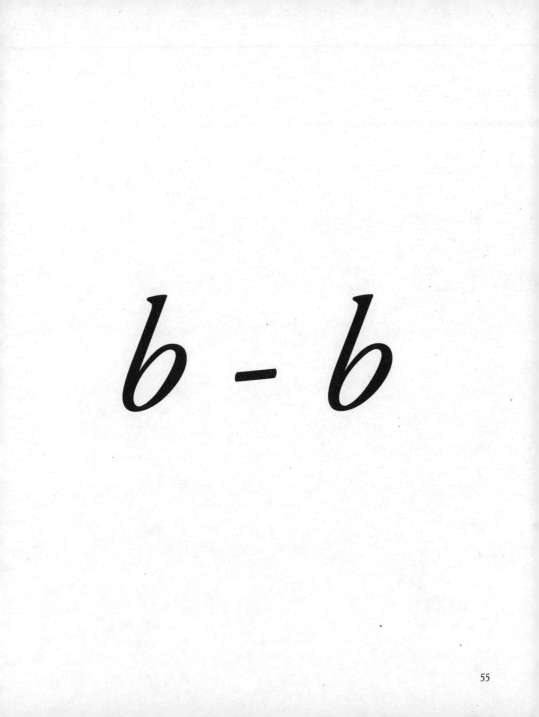

"Animal being opens up a space between manifestation and metaphysics, between appearance and the unconscious. Stated as formula, the animal can be pictured as being minus being, ~~being~~, or b minus b—pure negation."

—Akira Mizuta Lippit, *Electric Animal*

"To say we must be free of air, while admitting to knowing no other source of breath, is what I have tried to do here."

—Frank Wilderson, *Red, White & Black*

wade   in   the   water

wade   in   the   water   children.

wade   in   the   water

god's   gonna   trouble   the

water.

in   the   water. gonna   wade.   gonna   trouble.   gonna   children   in   the water. gonna water. gonna wade. gonna god's. in the water children wade. children water. children gods. in the water trouble water. trouble wade. trouble children. trouble gods in the water god's trouble. in the water god's children wade. in the water trouble gonna water the wading children of god. gonna trouble the children wading. gonna water the children in god's water. in the children's water gonna trouble the trouble. in the water the wading children are finished wading in the trouble. in the water the wading children gonna trouble the gods.

1

a child born in the water may take longer to
draw breath before they wake.

we often dream of flying, a kind of weightlessness that carries us up up up.
we know we are dreaming. outside the world of the dream we are afraid of
heights, careful to not look down, can feel our body mass; heavy. salt blood.
the people could fly, until they couldn't. salt kept us closer to the water. the
water is the birthplace of new world blackness.

blackness ain't just in the water.
blackness is the water.

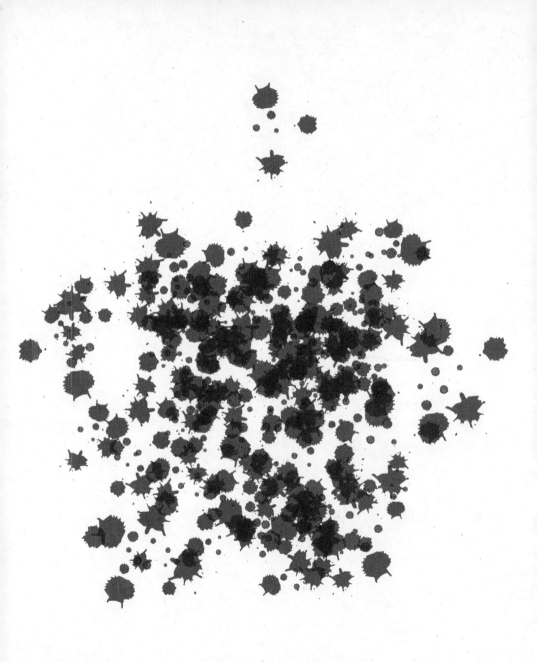

1 b - b

a **woman** miscarryed & the Child

~~dead within her~~

~~& Reason it~~ dyed

~~8 days after~~ delivery.

in which the fevered hands attend to the body
beguile asphyxiation of its abstract work.

Walcott taught us that the *sea is history*, that interwoven into the depths are countless stories, actual bones. there was a time when we had belief, when we were a believer in a kind of delivery, not this body, no, but something animating this flesh would be delivered. that the bones could be gathered. there was a time when we believed, when we, being delivered, had belief that we had been born again. there are many births, as there are many bellies of the world.

not a pending or imminent event but constitutive not a pending or imminent

we
are
the
sentient
dead.

2

our partner gave birth to our child, fully submerged in the water, the first few moments suspended. once removed from the water it took a while before the child would breathe, the doctor said this is normal, sometimes we wonder if black children are already aware of a world set on making their breathing an impossibility. we count so many years in the seconds before a first breath, something like a *living death*, a middle, passage. we name our child Ocean.

a breath-holding spell is a common event among young children. a breath-holding spell can be brought about when startled. sometimes children are startled. a breath-holding spell can bring a child in and out of consciousness.

wa ter \\'wôdᵊr, 'wädᵊr\\

water is the weather is the wake is the wade. water is the work is the wail is the world. in the wake of the body the baptism. in the wake is a world .

ontology—once
it is finally admitted
as leaving existence
by the wayside—
does not permit us
to understand
the ~~being~~ of the

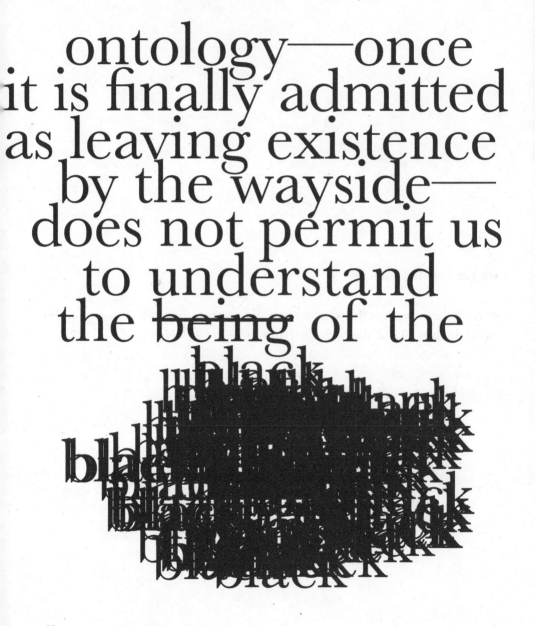

2 b – b

a woman miscarryed & the ~~Child~~

~~dead within~~ her

~~& Rotten~~ & ~~dyed~~

~~2 days~~ ~~delivery~~

see them collecting the oxygen, gathering it
against curated disaster. see their hands work

in 1675 Peter Blake would captain the James, a vessel that was to make its way to Barbados with what was to be described as cargo. held in the birthplace of new-world blackness, one of Glissant's *bellies of the world.* what is born from the hold of the ship is not alive. what is born from the hold of the ship is the sentient dead. abstracted to give shape to life. documented at the site of ruin.

Wake

WHEREIN PIP CONSIDERS ADVISING AHAB TO LOSE HIS HUMAN COORDINATES BUT JUMPS THE *PEQUOD* INSTEAD: MOVIE PITCH

SCENE BEGINS WITH PIP APPROACHING AHAB. a slow walk meant to dramatize the *longue durée* of silence, the absented speech that forms Pip's there and not thereness. the measured movements of contraband—each step an appeal to remain obscure— for the thing you are is smuggled. a secret open as the water. and then midway to Ahab, Pip gives attention to the sea, its sound—the applause of waves crashing against themselves—the din of the deep having its own syntactical order. and suddenly, without saying a word, language being a fraught thing, a jagged tool—Pip looks back only to offer a wry smile—and with no maps to guide them, Pip jumps the *Pequod*. back arched as a dorsal fin, marine opening up with the stammer of uncountable life forms shifting in and out of each other. and somewhere out in the blue basement of the earth, somewhere surrounded by that cold cellar with no more than the drink visible, Pip emerges like air and sound and all of that a world.

3

and how many moments are given to the child?
how long before the child is a body, never to wake?

Ocean cries a full-throated cry, a rattle, long and full. do not hold the child too tightly, do not squeeze them. we make assessments of a lifetime of danger, something like scanning the water for sharks. an English name for a "strange fish." a nomenclature developed by merchants over years on the water attempting to make an other so that the so-called human could hold its shape. *shark from "'xoc' pronounced 'choke,' from the Maya in the Caribbean."* we gasp, do not hold the child too tightly, there are sharks in the water.

this body is a fiction

...

what of the flesh?

strange fish
occupy the water.

3 b - b

~~a~~ woman ~~miscarryed~~ & ~~the~~ Child

~~dead within~~ her

       & ~~Poston~~ & **dyed**

~~6 days~~ after delivery.

to conceal a living body, one not meant to
survive. see a song, a lament, the willful work

in the book of mortality aboard the James, a constellation of disasters, an apocalypse by another name. in the ledger a child was said to be born, the body discoloured—*a child of the water*. in the dead book this discoloured body—*may take longer to draw*—is gone upon arrival, no possibility of *breath*. the body is a corpse Webster tells us. the child is but a body. in the book of mortality aboard the James the child is said to be born dead, the child is said to die two days later.

to be swallowed by
   the belly
   the end of the world
might be   a place
to begin.

to be

        of the whale

at the end

might be

4

is a child of the water, aboard the vessel,
a child at all? what is left in an un-child's wake?

what is left in the un-making of the child? which is to say, what is left in the un-making of childhood? when the rent is too high for us to find lodging there. this is not an argument around innocence, the child is not innocent—a hollow word—an imaginary border. the child is an ocean—which is to say—possible.

my body   given
              out,

...

the   animal.

my body   given
            distorted

...

     is   .

my body
was given back
to me sprawled out,

distributed

. . .

the Negro is an

animal

4 b - b

a ~~~~~~~~ ~~~~~~~~ ~~ the ~~Child~~

dead ~~within~~

              & Rotten & ~~dyad~~

2 ~~days after~~ delivery.

entangled with a journal of mortality.
one that only sees what is assumed: gone. its work

the question that compresses you is a matter of black life, the question is a matter of black death being an event or what constitutes blackness itself. if living aboard the mobile graveyard, it is to be in excess of this burial ground. if living it is to *steal breath* or *hide it*. blackness as excess is as close as you can approximate to otherwise, for to be alive— *through a passage the ledger cannot see—* on the floating tomb, is to be outside logic, is to be unimaginable, something without a grammar.

to

the end of the world
a place

to

world

5

who can rouse the breath like a mother? or hide it
like a hunted thing? a child is not a/wake.

breathe softer child, tuck our breathing beneath the water, though there be sharks there. make something of our body, itself a technology also. make a maroon, a saltwater wraith. make an underwater country Drexciya deep in the black atlantic. make our body part of the storm, unsettle the water.

sprawled out,

...

the Negro is

distorted

...

the   animal.

my body was

5 b - b

~~an ~~~~~~~~~miscarryed ~~&~~ ~~the~~ ~~Child~~

~~dead~~ ~~within~~ her

& **Rotten** & dyed

■ days after delivery.

to obscure in hollow numbers, to make vanish
in ditto dittos. see what is not said, out-work

the premature grammar of death. its cold logic
see, somewhere in the margins, the dead lungs, work.

you are long past believing in recovery, in believing there is something to be recovered—*snatch something from the water*—but what of letting the dead speak? what of the interstice of 48 hours where a presumed corpse may have had a hushed breath? there are no spells here for raising the dead. but there are dead speaking—wailing—as they wade in the water. this is not an attempt at resolution, this might be a failed attempt to work against it, to demand ellipsis of these fraught symbols. and what this be and ain't doesn't believe it can wretch an answer from the water, it is an ensemble of ontological questions— tucked in a wail—*that was meant for the wake.*

the dead are speaking, wailing above and
below the waterline.

and all that is breathing, all that is vibrating into something new.

6

wake the child while no one is looking, steal breath
through a passage the ledger cannot see. wake, wake

the child somewhere an account is not given. snatch
something from the water that was meant for the wake.

the child is more than a body, which is to say multiple, which is to say not reducible to a presumed corpse, something already drowned. ocean, in the deep, ocean, in the boundless parts, ocean, is more than a burial ground, a wake fixed in some linear fantasy of time, Ocean, at the end of the world, at the morning after it, a cry, whistling, carried on the wind, through the water, a wail song teaching us to breathe.

WHEREIN PIP CONCLUDES HIS BODY IS NOT SINGLE AND SELF-IDENTICAL. WHEREIN PIP DETERMINES HE IS ALSO THE WHALE, AND SWALLOWS THE *PEQUOD*: MOVIE PITCH

it is unclear where on the journey Pip decided a single body was unsuitable, but each day he would work depths of 40 feet, then 80 feet then twice that again. it begins by learning not so much to hold one's breath but how to better distribute the oxygen. a shrinking of the spleen, a releasing of oxygen-rich blood cells, one learns to slow the heart rate. one remembers something of their self that began in the water. what if the distance between the whale and the belly of the whale were imagined were nothing more than a myth? what if Pip could insist on other folk tales? on an assemblage of materials and temporalities continually passing through them? then it is not so much a stretch to say one relegated to silence, the speculative position of the non-human animal, is also the whale. that Pip could make new things of their body and swallow whole the things carrying the so-called old. it is unclear where on the journey Pip made these new things of his body, but who rides the *Pequod* when they can ride the ocean?

to be

to begin.

6 b - b

~~an accustom miscarryed~~ & the ~~Child~~

~~dead within~~ her

          & Rotten ~~is~~ dyed

2   ~~after~~ delivery.

perhaps this is all just a meditation on nothing. on breathing, on the shape of a clenched breath because some are perpetually consigned to be the antonym of life. what of the whale? what of the monstrous? what of leviathan, and to be in its belly? the black is not the whale, *the largest of which takes the biggest breaths on the planet* and can hold hold hold hold upwards of two hours. a knee. a neck. a chokehold. an expired breath. the black is not the whale. and the whale—dark thing that it is—is the whale and it must surface to breathe. and it is hunted at the surface, a place its ancestors once lived and gave up on too. the whale— dark thing that it is . . . is . . . is breathing and the air itself has become a toxic thing, a slow death. and perhaps this is all a meditation on bodies. and what they house. and who they be. and ain't. the whale and **in the belly of the whale.**

Work

in the end—which is a poor way to describe a point of departure—there was always already a connection to the water, to the thrashing body, its tremble and wail. inhale. in the end, when we say whale, it may just be an attempt at articulating a *spatiotemporality outside the human*, or any desire to be on the insides of that category. deep breath now. all of this matter is vibrating. all of this matter is less disciplined in its borders, undisciplined and without them. and deeper still. whale and ride the *alter-frequency*. wail and fold time. frustrate a supposed linearity. this ain't the end of the world. it's after that. in the end you are always already porous. nothing discrete. into this water, we commit this body—becoming something, somewhere else. always becoming. and from the water, something new—a too heavy grammar. in the end—the wail—another form of exhalation. breath and sound. wind and rattle. in the end—the wail—which is not to say the end of the wail, even if the end of the world. nah, after that. all of the bones have not been gathered, there is no gathering them all—& yet. and there is no recuperation to be found here—& yet. breathe deep again. enough air to hold us all. enough oxygen for multiple worlds. in the end, nah, after that and before it too. from the water—exhale—a wail song.

and . . . .

NOTES

this text, and any that I hope to write, is an attempt to hold an extended conversation with so many others. a web of ideas that have been carefully woven and manipulated here and which have yet to settle at the bottom of the ocean. the errors are my own, the oxygen is below.

"being itself, and its zero...which is to say blackness." For more on the "zero-degree position of non-value" for black being, see Calvin L. Warren, *Ontological Terror: Blackness, Nihilism, and Emancipation* (Durham, NC: Duke University Press, 2018) 40.

"the belly of the whale" is in conversation with Édouard Glissant's "belly of the world" in *Poetics of Relation*, trans. Betsy Wing (University of Michigan Press, 1997).

"distortions of distortion" again refers to the "zero degree position of non-value," a point of "saturation." See Warren, 76, 77.

"the Negro doing the double work of being border for the human and the animal." This is in conversation with the work of Zakiyyah Iman Jackson, especially with what Jackson has to say about the "centrality of the animal question for black existential matters." *Becoming Human: Matter And Meaning In An Antiblack World* (New York, NY: New York University Press, 2020) 19.

"name it something phallic" the sperm whale, gets its name due to the phallic-centric focus, which is to say the possessive focus, of those who saw the "cloudy" appearance of the liquid that shot from the head of the pierced whale. See Phillip Hoare, *The Whale: In Search Of The Giants Of The Sea* (New York, NY: HaperCollins Publishers, 2010) 65.

"no body here. a lit dinner, a lantern law." The free black—a paradox—was subject by law beginning in the early part of 18th century New York to lantern laws requiring that if they were to be out at night that their bodies be made visible by lantern, a lantern no doubt utilizing whale oil. For more on lantern laws see Simone Browne, *Dark Matters: On The Surveillance Of Blackness* Durham, NC: Duke University Press, 2015) 78-83.

The little I will say on Pip, a black character of Herman Melvilles' imagination who appears in Moby Dick is that this text referenced Pip on several occasions in an attempt, undoubtedly failed, to write against Melville and the black absented presence that haunted his mind. For more, which is to say: to ride the *Pequod* you can read Melville, the myth is here in the water.

"aboard some mobile graveyard." See Stephanie Smallwood, *Saltwater Slavery: A Middle Passage from Africa to American Diaspora.* "Slave ships were called tumbeiros in the eighteenth-century Angolan trade, for example, a term historians have translated as 'floating tombs' or 'undertakers.'" (137)

For more on *"seen but not seeing,"* see David Marriott's, *On Black Men.*

It was Sharon Patricia Holland's, *Raising The Dead: Readings of Death and (Black) Subjectivity*, that brought to light how "In *Webster's Ninth New Collegiate Dictionary*, the primary definition of the word body is 'corpse.' The secondary definition is 'person.'" (175)

"one is not a body / a discrete figure." When asked by Manthia Diawara what departure means to him, Edouard Glissant responds, "It's the moment when one consents not to be a single being and attempts to be many beings at the same time." Always this.

"one is a wail / falling." When a whale dies and is not washed ashore, the remains will eventually sink to the ocean floor. This is a whalefall. See Nick Pyenson, *Spying On Whales: The Past, Present, And Future Of Earth's Most Awesome Creatures.*

"peel a blanket / or two." In the processing of the whale's body, a cut would often be made below the blowhole and at strategic points to remove a large sheet of blubber. This was commonly called a blanket sheet. And as it often is with violence, name it something tender. See Eric Jay Dolin's, *Leviathan: The History Of Whaling In America.*

"& sometimes the great fish is brought to court." There was a time when the enlightened who sought to name and classify a whole world, thought that the whale was a fish, and someone who wanted to avoid taxes took the great fish to court to bring it into the fold of mammalia. This was not an effort to clarify classification, or to do less harm to a species, just a means to evade a fish-oil tax. See D. Graham Burnett, *Trying Leviathan: The Nineteenth Century New York Case That Put the Whale on Trial and Challenged the Order of Nature.*

"that ship my friends, was the first of recorded smugglers! The contraband was jonah." This is a direct quote from a sermon in Herman Melville's, *Moby Dick*, Macmillan Collector's Library edition, (86). "The contraband was Jonah." You are also now carrying contraband.

"because they can no longer breathe." See Frantz Fanon, *The Wretched Of The Earth*. "When we revolt it's not for a particular culture. We revolt simply because, for so many reasons, we can no longer breathe."

"as mad, a mad black thing." See Theri Alyce Pickens, *Black Madness :: Mad Blackness*.

"a body, itself both more and less than one." Here I am thinking of Moten, "what if embodiment enforces abstraction?" See *Stolen Life* by Fred Moten.

"your cognitive foil." See Frank Wilderson, *Afropessimism*. "I was the foil of Humanity. Humanity looked to me when it was unsure of itself. I let Humanity say, with a sigh of relief, 'At least we're not him.'" (13)

"preposition: the whale on land. who gave up on the land." See Dionne Brand, *Land To Light On*. "I don't want no fucking country, here or there and all the way back, I don't like it, none of it, easy as that. I'm giving up on land to light on." (48)

"dead reckoning." See Jack Whitten, Dead Reckoning I. Dead Reckoning, "the moment when a person sails out into the ocean so far that they can no longer tell where the land is."

the first 6 headers in the first numbered series are directly from Édouard Glissant's *Poetics of Relation*.

"this is the end of time, that shedding of the meaning of our bodies." This comes directly from Theri Alyce Pickens, *Black Madness :: Mad Blackness* (112)

"unthought and unrecognizable." See Saidiya Hartman and Frank B. Wilderson III. "The Position of the Unthought." *Qui Parle* 13, no. 2 (2003): 183-201.

"an animate entanglement of subject and object." For more on entanglement and the porousness of the perceived unified and singular body see Monique Allewaert, *Ariel's Ecology: Plantations, Personhood, and Colonialism in the American Tropics.*

"everything has vibration." See Ashon Crawley's essay, "Stayed / Freedom / Hallelujah", in the anthology *Otherwise Worlds: Against Settler Colonialism and Anti-Blackness.* "Everything living and dead, everything animate and immobile, vibrates. Vibration is the internal structuring logic of matter. Because everything vibrates, nothing escapes participating in choreographic encounters with the rest of the living world."

"a wail will use only a tiny amount of air to produce its click in the depths of the world." See the article published in *Scientific Reports*, "Deep-diving pilot whales make cheap, but powerful echolocation clicks with 50 uL of air." Illias Foskolos, Natacha Aguilar de Soto, Peter Teglberg Madsen, & Mark Johnson.

"and here we are in the nonworld of the singularity, the weather." See Christina Sharpe's, *In the Wake: On Blackness and Being* for her apt use of the weather as metaphor. Truly, the wake, is crashing through every sentence of *Wail Song*.

"and god created . . ." See Genesis 1:21.

"what is it to take seriously that some lives are not lived in the world that the world lives in." See Jared Sexton, "The Social Life Of Social Death: On Afro-Pessimism and Black Optimism." "Black life is not lived in the world that the world lives in."

"whales before, the before-whales." Prior to the epic proportions of their lives in the deep, the ancestors of whales, such as Pakicetus, walked on dry land. And then they gave up on land too. See Nick Pyenson, *Spying On Whales: The Past, Present, And Future Of Earth's Most Awesome Creatures.*

For the quote from Lippit, see *Electric Animal: Toward A Rhetoric Of Wildlife*

(51). For the quote from Wilderson, see *Red White & Black: Cinema and the Structure of U.S. Antagonisms* (338).

"1 b - b" each iteration of the erasures ending with b - b are drawn from the "Account of Mortallity of Slaves aboard the Shipp James" referenced in Stephanie Smallwood's, *Saltwater Slavery: A Middle Passage from Africa to American Diaspora* (139-142). A strange case where a child is referenced as being dead in the womb, and yet the description of the death and discoloration two days later as though the child has twice died or that there was a liminal period in which the child described as dead, lived. This story, of a chid born which died, a child born, by the cited untrustworthy account of mortality, dead and in death, is told by erasure here alongside the numbered series sans b - b which describes my own child by water birth, born submerged and initially, not breathing. These two threads are bookended by Wake and Work (see Christina Sharpe's, *In The Wake*). Partly as an unresolved (unresolvable?) question of what, if anything, can be recovered from the water, which in Sharpe's text, becomes a way of talking about the "afterlives of slavery."

"Walcott taught us that the sea is history." See Derek Walcott, *Another Life*.

"Ontology—once it is finally admitted as leaving existence by the wayside—does not

"what of the flesh?" Here I am thinking in conversation with and thinking about Hortense Spiller's reading of the flesh in, "Mama's Baby Papa's Maybe: An American Grammar Book."

"My body was given back to me sprawled out, distorted . . . the Negro is an animal." This is a direct quote from Fanon. See, *Black Skin, White Masks*.

"it is an ensemble of ontological questions." See Frank B. Wilderson III, *Red White & Black: Cinema and the Structure of U.S. Antagonisms*. "what is needed (for the Black, who is always already a Slave) is an ensemble of ontological questions that has as its foundation accumulation and fungibility as a grammar of suffering." (54)

Archive: After The End Of The World. "One body was not a sustainable unit for the project at hand. the project itself being black feminist metaphysics, which is to say, breathing." (6)

"Pip decided a single body was unsuitable." See Alexis Pauline Gumbs, *M Archive: After The End Of The World.* "One body was not a sustainable unit for the project at hand. the project itself being black feminist metaphysics, which is to say, breathing." (6)

"a shrinking of the spleen, a releasing of oxygen rich blood cells, one learns to slow the heart rate." For more on African swimming culture, and the body-alterations captives underwent while diving in the below, see Kevin Dawson, *Undercurrents of Power: Aquatic Culture in the African Diaspora* (65-67).

"the largest of which take the biggest breaths on the planet." For this reference and more on whales, and breath and a story the size of the world see Rebecca Giggs, *Fathoms: The World in the Whale.* "The biggest cetacean species possess Earth's most colossal lungs, and draw the planet's deepest breaths." (11) Jayna Brown, *Black Utopias: Speculative Life and the Music of Other Worlds.* "I suggest that we see and feel our way not into a future but into an altogether different spatiotemporality that is not discoverable along a human timeline." (8) and "The versions of utopia I explore involve relationalities that radically disrupt the very idea of the future, as they tune into an alter-frequency." (8)

and . . .

ALWAYS ACKNOWLEDGEMENT

i want to thank *The Rumpus* and *HERE Poetry Journal*, specifically Carolina Ebeid and Jay Labbe for your invitations to share earlier iterations of this extended thinking. Douglas Kearney, Lara Mimosa Montes, fahima ife, and Sun Yung Shin, your early readings and feedback, your questions, and the generous words you've offered up were instrumental, thank you, thank you always. to Lillian Yvonne-Bertram, so grateful for your work in the world and for pulling me in to have this work wade in Black Ocean, ya'll were first on my list and so grateful for the care you, Janaka Stucky, Carrie Adams, Taylor Waring, and Charlotte Rener brought to this.

and there are so many more that could be named, the network of thinking both in and outside my body, our bodies but i will just extend my thanks to the water & to Christina Sharpe & Dionne Brand whose work has taught me so much about the outsideness of time . . .